*For Jennifer, Adam and Amy*
*C.H.*
*For Rachel and Carolyn*
*F.K.*

First published in 1992
Text copyright © J.M. Dent & Sons, Ltd, 1992
Illustrations copyright © Claire Henley, 1992

The right of Claire Henley
to be identified as the Illustrator of this work has been asserted by
her in accordance with the Copyright, Designs and Patents Act 1988.

Text by Fiona Kennedy and Jane Heslop.

Printed in Italy
for J.M. Dent & Sons Ltd
91 Clapham High Street
London SW4 7TA

Photoset by Deltatype Limited, Ellesmere Port

A catalogue for this book is available from the British Library.

The illustrations for this book were prepared using gouache paints.

# OCEAN DAY
# Claire Henley

Dent Children's Books

London

Waves lap the yellow sand.
Seaweed and shells are stranded
on the shore.

Lazy green turtles bask in the sun.
The sea is calm.

Dolphins leap and twist in
the dark blue waves.

Watch that diver!
He swims deeper and deeper
down to the ocean bed.

Tiny rainbow-coloured fish
dart to and fro in the coral reef.

Jelly fish glide.
A long-legged octopus
swirls and twirls.

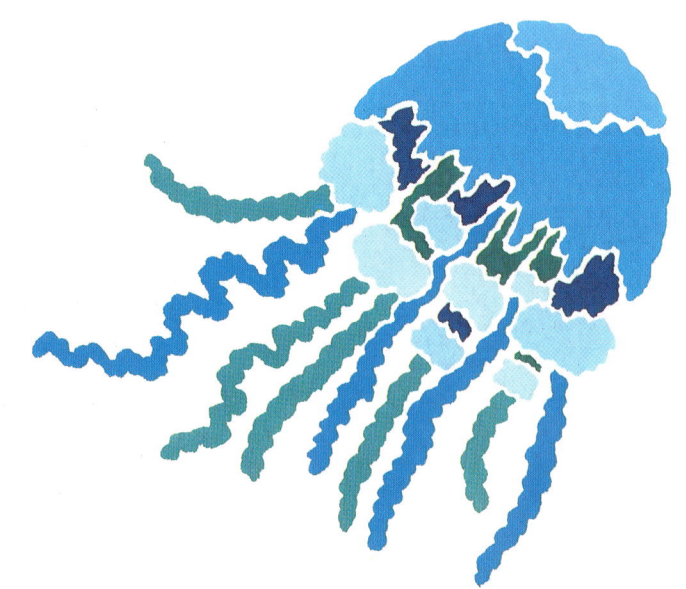

Seahorses and starfish float past.
Sea-anemones ripple in the warm water.

In the harbour
a ship is ready to sail
to distant stormy seas.

Gulls wheel and scream over
the foaming water.
They are looking for food.

Huge whales spout
fountains of icy water high
into the sky.

Smart penguins with
bright orange beaks dive off
jagged icebergs.

The voyage is nearly over.
The captain and crew set a
course for home.